Secret Grief

Cathryn Deyn

Copyright © 2018 Cathryn Deyn

All rights reserved, including the right to reproduce this book, or portions thereof in any form. No part of this text may be reproduced, transmitted, downloaded, decompiled, reverse engineered, or stored, in any form or introduced into any information storage and retrieval system, in any form or by any means, whether electronic or mechanical without the express written permission of the author.

The views expressed in this work are solely those of the author and do not necessarily reflect the views of the publisher, and the publisher hereby disclaims any responsibility for them.

ISBN: 978-0-244-08889-7

PublishNation
www.publishnation.co.uk

In loving memory of all those we miss.

Foreword

The woman talks, a mixture of sadness, confusion and rage.

She is reluctantly letting go of a friendship, but she is letting go screaming, because she doesn't understand how, or why it is over.

She's expressing grief, though she would never have used that word, because no-one has died.

But then, as Cathryn reveals in this wonderful book, bereavement takes many forms. It may be the life-stopping death of a loved one... or the children leaving home. It may be a dream of ours coming to nothing; the loss of a job, the end of a friendship or diminishing health.

There's so much to let go of as the years unfold, and in these emotionally literate pages, we are invited beyond the happiness bias, in which everything must be shiny and positive, towards the hidden lakes, the more wounded aspect of our pysche, and towards a kind of self-honesty, the most healing path of all.

Through rage, through creation, through darkness, through avoidance, through denial, through kindness, through numb, through sadness, through love, through joy, through insensitivity, through judgement, through a growing understanding of ourselves and our 'one precious life' ... Cathryn leads us with poetry and understanding.

Rather than speak of the stages of grief, I learn to speak only of today. 'This is how I feel, and it's allowed'. I find myself on a journey, though not as the crow flies. And as long as I stay honest, allowing my life to rise and fall within me, and kind, allowing punishing thoughts to pass - I'll be fine.

Grief is rejection, grief is abandonment, and with care, grief is invitation. It cuts like a cold wind, it deadens like a sodden blanket, it maims like a car out of control...and is a door, always a door, a fresh starting for ourselves.

And wherever I am today, (and no inner state is a crime) there will be a poem in this book for me.

Simon Parke

Author of *One Minute Mindfulness* and other books.

www.simonparke.com

Contents

Introduction		1
Chapter 1	Your Space	5
	Tips for Journaling	7
	Journal pages	10
Chapter 2	The Whole Picture	13
	The Poetry	15
	Truth	16
	The L Word	17
	Pandora's Box	18
	The Clown	19
	Clearing	20
	Let's	21
	Journal pages	22
Chapter 3	The Happiness Bias	25
	Innate Intelligence	28
	Glances	30
	Gang	31
	Out	33

Chapter 4	Facing The Unthinkable	34
	Broken Pots	36
	Adjusting	37
	Fulcrum	39
	The Secret	41
	The Edge	43
	Hidden	44
	Interred	45
	How	47
	Marmalade	49
	Tired	50
	Waves	52
	L'Enfant	54
	Lesson	55
	Solo	56
	Platitudes	57
	Waiting	59
	This Farewell	61
	Keepsakes	62
	In Time	64
	Unreal	65
	Support Group	66
	Guilt	67
	Impossible	68
	Fantasy	70

Neolithic	72
Maybe One Day	74
Incognito	75
Hindsight	77
Resistance	79
Bottomless	80
All Around	81
In Memoriam	82
Mirror	83
Fool Proof	84
Dressing Up	86
Regeneration	87
Revelation	88
Stages	89
One Way	91
Absence	92
Before	94
Daffodils	96
Dinner Party	97
Cold Spell	99
Lido	101
Half Baked	103
Origami	104
It's Time	105
Embodied	107

~ Journal Page ~

~ Journal Page ~

Chapter 2

The Whole Picture

There are many poems in this book about bereavement, for obvious reasons, but of course, we face the loss of many things.

We can lose a home, a job, a friendship or relationship for other reasons besides death. Hopes, dreams and plans can die. We can lose our sense of identity because of changes in life circumstances. We may lose our health. We can feel desolate when our children leave home and a new phase of our life begins before we are ready for it. Ageing can also bring a sense of grief, as we face the inevitable changes in our bodies, and our own mortality. We can grieve for the pain of another person too, as we empathise with those we love, and in our basic human compassion for the suffering of others. As human beings we have a lot of loss to handle!

We may appear from the outside to be moving smoothly enough through our life. We keep our head above water and manage reasonably well yet are secretly aware all the while of things that nudge at us from within...things we would rather ignore because they feel daunting. Losses that we have been stoical about, and never fully faced.

Our ability to detach from our emotions is often impressive and can be very useful in the short term, but if we remain unrelentingly stiff upper-lipped we can spend a lifetime knowing ourselves only a little. We will suffer untold stress as we keep a tight rein on ourselves, believing that to feel things fully is not a desirable or constructive thing to do.

In fact, to feel fully is to live fully.

The things we hide from ourselves can be the things we most need to see...

~

The Poetry

How strange
the human countenance.
How neat, how tidy is the
face, the skin, the parcelling up
of a world too huge to understand.

Within us all, a universe of self,
yet there is no door upon which
to knock; no way in. We circle each
other like polite planets, wave
hopefully across the void.

Within us, music plays.
Giant, crashing symphonies
remain unheard, unsung, unpublished.

Rip-tide currents swirl and pull; the stirrings
of each soul. The poetry, oh the poetry
of each beating heart.

Truth

I am the light of a thousand moons,
I am the swell of an angry tide,
I am the calm that gives birth to a storm,
I am a shell with the ocean inside.

I am the beat of a wounded heart,
I am the wings of a captive bird,
I am the air in the lungs of a new-born,
I am a cry that has never been heard.

I am the teeth in the mouth of a tiger,
I am a crack in the wall of a dam,
I am a thread in the eye of a needle,
I am the lion that lies with the lamb.

I am a salmon that battles the currents,
I am the luminous lustre of pearl,
I am the lure of the distant horizon,
I am a cliff face, the edge of the world.

The L Word

When loss arrives, life is changed. Our greatest challenge is not experiencing the loss itself, but learning how to survive it, adjust to it and face the truth of our own responses to it. As we are forced to live a different life following a great loss, we can remain forever shocked, like rabbits in the headlights of that event, unless we help ourselves (and allow ourselves to be helped) to gradually come to terms with things – not just in our logical minds, but as whole beings.

The truth of life can be so bitter, so harsh. We have no power to reverse it externally. Internally though, dwells that which we can use to overcome just about anything... *our own truth.* Allowed to surface, it will protect us, cocoon us and heal us. As we recoil in shock away from loss, we are wise to trust our instincts to go within. It is here that our truths are waiting, ready to do the job they are designed for; to carry us through the shadows and out into the light of living again...

Pandora's Box

It took courage
you said,

to crawl into
the darkest depths
of yourself

and feel your way
around,

but as your eyes
adjusted to
the gloom,

you saw that
it was simply
beautiful.

The Clown

Don't paint on a smile
for me; in fact, let me
wipe away those giant
ruby lips, and I will kiss
the sadness I find
underneath.

Don't put on a show
for me; all that false jollity
is hiding something
far more precious.
Your silence
is golden.

Don't be the life and
soul of the party; be the
life and soul of your own
sweet and loving self.
It is more than
enough.

Clearing

Go
beyond
your fear,

for if you
only knew it,
fear is fog.

Yes-blinding,
thick and
dense,

but reach
out your hand
and feel the truth.

There is
nothing in
your way.

Let's

Let's not pretend
that life is a picnic.
That we skip through
a sea of red gingham
with wicker baskets.

Let's not bury our heads
in the sands of false optimism
and ignore the cries of those
above ground.

Let's be realistic.
Let's confront the loss
and the suffering, and look
it squarely in the eye.

Let it know who's boss.
Let it know we always laugh
after we cry.

Let's rise to the challenge
of telling our truths.

Let's.

~ Journal Page ~

How do I deal with my feelings at the moment?

Do I distract myself to avoid my feelings, and if so, how?

What is it like if I allow myself to notice what is going on inside of me?

What are some of my inner truths?

~ Journal Page ~

~ Journal Page ~

Chapter 3

The Happiness Bias

What we hunger for more than anything else is to be known in our full humanness, yet that is often what we fear most. It is important to tell the secret of who we truly and fully are, even if we only tell it to ourselves...otherwise we run the risk of losing track of who we are and come to accept the highly edited version we put forth in hope that the world will find it more acceptable than the real thing. Telling our secrets makes it easier for other people to tell a secret or two of their own, and exchanges like that have a lot to do with what being a family, and being human is all about.

Frederick Buechner

We humans lean towards happiness the way that plants lean towards sunlight. This seeking of loveliness is completely understandable. It feels good! At first glance it would seem to be a wholly commendable strategy to live our lives with a positive attitude and a determination to see the glass always as half-full. However, with such a happiness bias, we are attempting to ignore half of ourselves, and half of *life* itself.

We tend to turn away from pain. We do not want to think about or experience the shadow sides of our internal and external realities, and hence try to relegate our emotional distress signals to some place out of sight, mind and body. We strive to live like 'shiny happy people' and are somehow ashamed to be anything other.

Unfortunately, in doing so we miss many crucial messages – our 'negative' feelings are emotional 'red flags' that naturally spring up from within and are designed to guide, protect and heal us.

There is a huge misunderstanding that negative emotions such as anger, are bad for us. In fact, it is the 'internal pressure cooker' effect of their *suppression* that has a damaging impact upon the physical body. Processing feelings safely, objectively and therapeutically can dramatically improve our health.

In normal circumstances, the happiness bias is simply an insidious nuisance, but when loss crashes into our life it can be disastrous. We can feel ashamed of our own grief, convinced we must be weak, lazy, cowardly, pessimistic, ungrateful and deficient in some strange way, simply because we feel so unhappy.

We blame ourselves for not trying hard enough to be happy, when the real problem is that we are not allowing ourselves to be sad.

Our vulnerabilities and instinctive fears are an integral part of us as whole human beings. They complete a beautiful circle of emotional function. Escaping from the gilded prison of the happiness bias we can gain in psychological strength and emotional competency, learn to navigate through all our responses and come to feel more grounded and truly present in the world.

Life is much more satisfying when we no longer spending half of the time avoiding ourselves!

Innate Intelligence

Our life force, via the brain/body feedback system, controls and oversees the vast number of physiological processes in the body. We can consciously 'interfere with' some of those processes. For example, we can choose to hold our breath if we want to, but if we do this for too long it becomes extremely uncomfortable due to the build-up of carbon dioxide in our blood, and our body's unconscious desire to survive will compel us to breathe.

It makes sense to me that our minds/bodies have a 'healing manifesto' for grief and that our grief builds up in a very similar way when we resist it with our will.

Eventually we are forced to notice the unpleasant feelings as they have accumulated to an intolerable degree. This is the longer and harder way to grieve. If we spent all day trying not to breathe each breath, we would be utterly exhausted by dinner time! Resisting our innate need to grieve drains us of energy in a very similar way.

Just as we trust and rely on our inner intelligence to 'breathe us', so too can we learn to let it 'grieve us' through traumatic loss.

~

*Grief can be the garden of compassion.
If you keep your heart open through everything,
your pain can become your greatest ally in
your life's search for love and wisdom.*

Rumi

Glances

Beyond a
shadow of
a doubt

there is a place
where certainty
can be seen,
glinting,

but like sunlight
bouncing from
a mirror,

it hurts to
look.

Gang

I saw them today -
my unmet needs, and gosh
there were a lot of them.

In fact, there was a whole crowd
of them coming towards me
up the street.

I ran indoors, locked the door
and peered through
the letterbox.

They all marched past, looking
for me. I didn't even breathe
until the last one was gone.

I hope they don't
come back.

*

They must have gotten wise to me,
my unmet needs. They loiter on the
corner, all chatting and nonchalant,
as if they have all the time
in the world.

They seem to know where
I live now, and I need
to buy milk...

*

Well, they really surprised me,
my unmet needs. They just
stepped aside as I barrelled past
with my head down.

One of them offered to carry
my shopping, and so I invited
them all home for a cup of tea.

It was funny, but once we got
talking, it was if I'd known
them all for years.

Out

I walk in changing weather,
soon in wind and rain.

Feel!
insist these great elements
of earth's breath and ocean.

They breach wool and leather,
finding my thin skin beneath.

Feel!
they urge as I shrink
and shiver, and run towards home
with its' warmth and comfort.

But I wonder as I run,
what it is I run from.

How great is the storm?
How wild are the elements of me;
what hurricane do I stow away within?

Chapter 4

Facing The Unthinkable

There is a sacredness in tears. They are not the mark of weakness, but of power. They speak more eloquently than ten thousand tongues. They are the messengers of overwhelming grief, of deep contrition, and of unspeakable love.

Washington Irving

It is so painful to sit with our grief but providing ourselves with authentic grieving space is one way we can take care of ourselves when we are dealing with loss.

Time out is vital. It helps us to adjust. It makes 'putting on the brave face' when we must, less exhausting and helps us to recharge our batteries and carry on with everyday life.

Grieving space means time to 'flop'. To just be yourself, however you are feeling. Unless we make this space for ourselves, recovery will be slower and more difficult.

We may need to live this way for quite a while. Authentic and lasting adjustment to great loss cannot be achieved hurriedly, nor simply with willpower. Our brains, hearts and bodies require specific and gentle care as they adjust to the new situation. The more we can allow nature to take its' course, the smoother will be our journey to the other side of grief.

Ideally, we should not have to do this healing alone. Finding support is incredibly important. When we talk to other people who understand and perhaps also seek professional help, we are offsetting the innate sense of loneliness that great loss creates. Being seen and heard properly soothes the heart, relaxes the body and increases our sense of security and belonging. Facing the unthinkable should not have to be our own private hell. At least, not all the time!

~

Broken Pots

They said it would come,
this winter's gale. A vast
Nordic chill, roaring through,
forcing itself into small spaces
with mean efficiency.

I do not see it happen, but
the pieces tell a story. Shards of
sun-bleached terracotta, strewn
across the freezing ground.

This scouring of a gentle place.
This bleakest interlude.

Adjusting

For you are gone
and I am not.
This fact is cold
and hard as
stone;

to live with it
my only option,
and there is no
handy manual
for that.

Becoming used
to the sharpness
is like breathing
needles, so I hold
my breath.

It will soften in time
they say, in some
imaginary white
washed future.

There I will smile
at the memories, and
find my gladness all
crumpled and in need
of laundering.

Fulcrum

The world turns in one second,
and becomes in that second,
my nemesis.

In this place I do not know,
all familiar things are changed.
Nothing escapes the brush of
loss, the sweep of a colour
I cannot name.

Looking down, I see
a tightrope stretched from
past to future, along which
I must travel.

There is no return to
solid ground. I cannot
jump down and laugh and
realise it was just a game –

only in my dreams, when
those I lost, wave at me and
I wave back and relief floods
through my sleeping veins.

Loss can infiltrate every fibre of your being, and every atom of your reality. Until such a loss happens there is no way of understanding how completely all-consuming the experience of it can be.

The Secret

He turns it over
in his mind.

A shiny coin with
two sides.

He cannot know
which way it would
fall, should he flip it
and chance his life
to its' whim.

They may smile and
applaud him with open
faces, or turn away;
close hearts and doors.

He turns the coin
again, again, the secret
shinier by the minute.

Sharing our inner secrets can be so difficult, especially if we have been betrayed or wounded by others in the past. The burden of an untold secret can be immense. Find a person with whom you feel safe, to confide in. A secret released, can set you free.

The Edge

When life falls away
beneath my feet and crumbles
like white chalk into an ocean that
pounds the rocks beneath me -
at this great cliff edge, let me learn
from sea birds, that with grace,
lift off from a nested ledge and
ride great pillows of air
softly down onto
the water.

Hidden

Hurt
makes a vixen
of me.

I pull away
into the shadows
of myself,

to lick the wounds
of my soul.

Interred

I wonder where they go to die -
all the wasted opportunities.

The ones we fail to acknowledge, with
our heads stuck in the sand or up our bums.

Somewhere, there must be a huge graveyard.
I'd like to visit and take flowers, for my sorrow
and my not noticing.

Maybe we all have our own sections, and
would look in horror at all we have let slip by,
and weep over blemished marble.

Or perhaps opportunities really belong to no-one,
and lie in unmarked graves, and we would wander
vague amongst them, little moved and none the wiser.

Times of loss are often clouded with regret. Hindsight drags us back to moments we would now choose to handle in a different way. Some people advise we should 'regret nothing', yet our regrets are simply a measure of how much we have changed and grown through our experiences. Sadness about some of our choices is an unavoidable side effect of emotional maturity, but we can be compassionate with ourselves for making mistakes and being a fallible human being.

How

How is it
that when you left,
you disappeared like
a footprint in a sand dune.

How did the world spill into
your space like water, as if you
were never there, when inside
of me a canyon was suddenly
hewn out, a million years of
geology in an instant.

I find myself stranded between
those walls, watching birds, just dots,
crossing a blue eternity above,

while someone else sits in your
seat and the earth does
not screech to a halt.

How is this?

Our minds love the familiar. When change comes we are confused and bewildered. The brain looks for old patterns and finds only different ones. This time of adaptation feels unbelievable and dream-like, and everything is a question.

Marmalade

I don't care for it,
with its' lurking peel
and strange acidity,
but you did.

Exclusively yours, it still hogs
the middle of the top shelf,
waiting for toast time and
supper crumpets.

Life, you said, is marmalade.
Sweet yet bitter, all at the same time.
I wish you had taken it with you, this jar
of deep philosophy, but you forgot to
pack it; maybe you were hurting too.

I reach for the honey; organic, cold-pressed,
made by heather-fed bees who roam wild moors.
I help myself. Savour the gentle illusion.
Revel in the false promises of
golden honeycomb.

Tired

Grief has wrung
me out.

A damp cloth, I am
hung out to dry.
I flop this way and that
in a lacklustre breeze.

Friends call with the best ideas,
but they all sound to me
like climbing the Alps
without boots.

Rest then, they say, but if
I sleep, I may be gone for
a month.

Eyelids, limbs, bones
drooping. Am I melting?
I nod off like a child, in
the middle of my lunch.

It takes an enormous amount of energy to adjust to traumatic loss. There are times when the tiredness will seem out of all proportion to circumstances. It will come and go and can be confusing and frustrating. Trust your body. Sleep allows healing and integration of the difficult new reality.

Waves

It comes up;
a tsunami they call it,
of grief.

Turns me to matchsticks.
I float amongst debris,
no longer recognisable,
even to myself.

In a dry spell, I work hard
to rebuild some semblance
of normality.

It is always a shock.
It comes up once more.
A tsunami they call it,
of grief.

Emotional energy comes naturally in waves. When we know this, we can more easily ride out the times of intensity as we grieve and make the most of the quieter periods in between. When emotion surges again, we have not 'regressed'.... it is just another wave passing through.

L'Enfant

My grief is a different grief.
A grief so hard to comprehend,
for you were never here.

I hoped for you, planned for you.
My heart reserved a place for you,
trusting in your beautiful reality.

You never came, and now you
are gone.

Wherever you are, out there on
the breeze, in the surge of a great
river, in the green tips of new-born leaves;
in whatever form your spirit moves through
this world, you are still mine to miss.

I blow a kiss into the sky,
hoping it will float like a feathered seed,
and land softly in your soul.

Lesson

Let me take my pain
and make of it
an arrow,

and place it to mark
the wisest path,

so, should I pass
this way again,

I will remember
the point of it.

Solo

No-one understands.
Not really.

No-one is this me,
losing you.

These are not histrionics.

As if I would choose to plumb
these extraordinary
depths, alone.

Platitudes

Look on the bright side
they tell me, as if one
should be easy to find.

I turn events over and over
in my mind. Nope.
No bright side to
be seen.

Maybe one will pop
up like toast.

I wish one would.

I'm starving.

Sometimes the flippancy of platitudes can be useful to us, helping us stay on the surface of our feelings, and skim along more lightly. Sometimes, when other people use them they can be infuriating and depressing! Such is the paradoxical experience of loss...

Waiting

time
like molten
glass, stretches and is
changed; minutes drawn
out, tear-shaped,
fragile

~

moments
stretched, become
thin slivers of reality
denying passage to
the gathered
grains
of
s
a
n

d

My father Ken died aged 51, after a two-year struggle with cancer. We had been ever hopeful that against all odds he would somehow miraculously defy his terminal diagnosis. His last weeks changed things. We were now waiting for the inevitable and for the end of pure suffering. Time was both a curse and a blessing - the torturer and yet the provider of those most precious final days.

This Farewell

She is tired tonight, and
the soft white of her hair
delicate, as if spun on an
angels loom.

The clock is ticking,
I swear more softly, as it tiptoes
with respect through the hours,
each second more profound
than the one before.

I watch her flutter.
She is a wisp upon
the breeze.

I hear her laughing as the
room brightens.

Somewhere just beyond
where I can be now, it is dawn
and a hundred thousand bells
begin to peal.

Keepsakes

I am guardian of
a lost life.

It is hidden in a small box
on a high shelf. It gathers dust
that I blow away; watch dancing
in the air on sunny days.

She has been gone too long.
No-one bar me lifts the lid and
welcomes her back into this pale world.

She brings the colour of her cheeks,
the gloss of her hair. She sparkles
in rectangle memories, looks at me
through a long-gone lens.

Yes, I was here! she laughs.
I lived well and full, didn't I?

It is so hard to put her away;
to make her tidy and cover
her smile.
Some days I leave
her all over the desk.

On other days I cannot bear
to visit. She waits, ever smiling,
and I am driven half-mad by
her patient silence.

In Time

I was not ready.
How could I have been, while
you were still here, breathing?

A world without you was an
unknown planet, simply inconceivable.

I am waiting.
Now that you have vanished, I am
wondering when I will allow you not to be here;
when my heart will not demand to see you soon.

It must come one day, the loosening of these ties.
A moment when I will let you slip into the
flowing stream of the universe, bless you
on your voyage, trust in your
grand adventures without me.

I am thinking of it, at least.
Being ready.

One day.

Unreal

I expect you, as if you
have not left at all, which
makes it harder.

A rational sliver of me
remembers you are gone.
Other bits of me bumble
along, unknowing.

I wish they would hurry up
and get with the program.

I wish they would stop laying
you a place at dinner time.

Support Group

Elsie Baker's been to salsa.
Mrs Johnson's booked a cruise.
Patrick's flown to San Francisco.
I can barely even move.

Even among a group of other people who know how grief feels, we are often acutely aware of the individual differences. Our own pace can be a lonely one for sure.

Guilt

A splash of tea
falls onto crisp, white linen
and spreads like blood in snow.
I stare wide-eyed and mortified;
a rabbit in the headlights of faux-pas.

It's nothing! you cry, but your face
begs to differ. You dab and dab.
I hold back my breath and
blink faster.

The blot will likely stain.
Some things are fixed forever.
Some things just cannot be undone.

We can harbour guilty feelings like toxic waste. Constant self-recrimination achieves nothing. Forgiving ourselves for our 'tablecloth stains' is the far wiser option.

Impossible

I must let you go
they intimate, often,
as if you are a pebble
I might drop into a pond.

Let you go, how?

The you who is woven
into the very fabric of me;
the thread I dare not pull at
lest I unravel completely.

You must accept they say,
and pat my arm.

As if you are a feather
I could cast into the breeze;
as if you are just one beat
of this lonely, aching heart.

Such well-meaning advice can have unfortunate ramifications. Trying to 'let go' often results in a stuffing down of feelings. There is not a special switch we can press to achieve true acceptance. Our heart is simply asking to be allowed to feel what it feels, for as long as it needs to feel it.

Fantasy

How I wish someone
could see through my
pretences; spot the real me
quivering in long grass
and dive in, hawk-like.

Whisk me up, away into
the clouds, so I need do
nothing, just dangle,
trusting my fate.

How I wish someone
would scythe through
the burbled nonsense I
hear myself speaking, and
tie me up in a neat bundle.

Stack me with others who
need to lean, and leave us
under tarpaulin, for the whole
winter of this grieving season.

How I wish someone
might know, without
having to ask.

See, with one glance
into my eyes, how I long
to fall, to surrender,
to succumb.

Neolithic

Today is a Survival Day.
I made it official.
I breathe.
I eat, sometimes.
I do not brush my hair.

There is no such thing
as housework, or making
an extra effort.

On Survival Days, I
legitimately sleep, as
the world honks and
fusses outside.

In the mirror is a cave-dweller.
I tell her she is beautiful, that
she has a smear of jam on her
chin, that tomorrow might
be different.

I give her the thumbs up.
We both agree.
Survival Days rock.

Sometimes just existing is effort enough. The odd survival day/week/month can pay rich dividends, helping us adjust to loss without the constant external pressures of everyday life. They should perhaps be available on prescription!

Maybe One Day

I wish I was brave enough.
Wise enough, robust enough.
Calm enough, philosophical enough.
Patient and gentle and clever enough.

I wish I was consistent enough.
Inventive enough, understanding enough.
Cynical enough, smart enough.
Creative and cool and collected enough.

To handle it, to rise above it.
To navigate it, skilfully process it.
To cope with it, be virtually unfazed by it.
To graciously and gracefully accept it.

But I'm not.
Yet.

Incognito

I should be over it
she says, as she counts
the years, and wonders
why she is still not who
she used to be.

Where did I go? she asks,
as she catches a glimpse of
someone strange in the
mirrors' depths.

She lost him, and herself also.
Nobody seems to notice the imposter
in her place, who wears her clothes and
drives her car so expertly;

who rustles up her signature bakes
as if she is not a recent arrival who must
study the recipes in secret, and cannot
remember how they should taste at all.

Grief can create a very peculiar feeling ...'who am I?' So much of the familiar has vanished. On looking at the world now we do not have the usual references, the ones we have defined ourselves by. It takes time to create a new sense of self, and this is truly disconcerting.

Hindsight

I understand now
how hard it is to smile
when your heart is broken.

How it takes all you have
left to switch the kettle on,
journey to the fridge for milk.

I understand now why there
was silence, why you seemed
distant, why you did not call.

How natural it feels to seek
a private cave in which to mend.
How lonely that cave can feel
when no-one comes.

I understand now, why small
kindnesses mean so much, why
they seem as rare as snow
in summer.

I will move now, more thoughtfully
through this world. I send my love
back through time, to knock
upon your door.

It is only when deep grief consumes us that we can get a truer glimpse of how hard it has been for others dealing with their losses. Until we feel it ourselves, we simply do not know.

Resistance

There was a young fool
who made it a rule, to
carry, in autumn,
some glue.

He pasted the leaves,
back onto the trees,
for he felt it the
right thing to do.

If only we could go back. Do it again. Stop it happening. Get it right. Relish it more. If only we could start again. If only loss would bugger off and not exist!

We all have If-only-itis sometimes.

Bottomless

I worry that my grief
is a well, into which
I shall topple.

And fall, like Alice.
And fall, and fall.

And that this will be
my life hereafter.

Even as I think of it,
I wobble.

How uncertain
is this spinning earth
beneath my feet.

Grief is not a bottomless well, but it certainly looks like one from the top...

All Around

Your being gone is harder
for the shocking strangeness
of the space.

I did not think of space before.
My eyes were fixed on all the bright,
shiny stuff of this world, of which
you were a part.

Not once did I see the gaps
between words, hear silence between
notes of music, nor understand how real
they are. Not once did I truly notice
your absences, or wonder at the
quietness as you slept.

A tree I knew was felled recently.
I mourned it as a friend, for I loved it.
I wish I could have loved the spaces
between its' branches, for
they were not felled.

They are exactly where
they always were.

In Memoriam

I would carve your name on every bench.
Engrave it on every trophy.
Fly it on every flag.

I would advertise it on every hoarding.
Print it on every magazine cover.
Plant it out in every flower bed
and wait for you to bloom.

Mirror

I wear my distress
like weathered beech.

I am older, carved by
the hand of loss, into
twisted shapes.

Tears have worn
smooth, deep channels
in my soul.

My pain flows through
them, a great underground
river; a hidden wonder
of this world of me.

Fool-Proof

I am tired of crying.
Bored, bored, bored.
The next thing I know
I'm making paella
from scratch.

Now I know,
to grieve myself
bored. It works
every time.

If we allow ourselves to feel the way we feel, with absolutely no holds barred, a surprising thing happens. For a while the feelings intensify and then they will lessen and lift. It is physiologically impossible to sustain a pure emotion for very long. Try it. Identify a specific emotion. Then, be more depressed than you are. Be angrier than you are. Be sadder than you are. Allow the wave of it to get bigger. Invite more… and see what happens next.

Dressing Up

I found a box,
and in it were luxurious garments,
and the labels said, "Courage and Wisdom" XL.

I draped them around me, like a lady in fine furs
and paraded in front of a long mirror.

I rather liked the way they looked,
and wondered if I might
grow into them.

Regeneration

Change comes
and is not subtle.
It bulldozers through
the world you built with
such concerted efforts.

You must stand aside
or be flattened under
caterpillar wheels.

Life is levelling for new
foundations. It just didn't
consult you first.

Revelation

My heart spoke to me.

This sadness, it said,
is a measure of my
capacity to love.

Stages

There was no audition.
Life simply cast me in
this starring role.

I do my best with shock, denial
and anger, but the audience
grow restless, look at their
watches.

By the time I reach sadness
they have all gone home.

If a tree falls in the forest
when no-one is there,
does it make a sound?

We are social creatures, with a built-in need to be seen and heard. If we are not, we can feel as if we do not exist, and loneliness happens. Loneliness is an internal emotional prompt to seek connection, but in grief we are often frozen through shame and/or mistrust.

At times like this, acknowledging ourselves can help a great deal – this means becoming our own attentive audience. It is quicker than waiting for help it to arrive from other people! It can also be can be a valuable first step in building the confidence to reach out to others.

Journaling is an excellent way to witness our own experiences...

One Way

I am full of emotion.
Round and fat with it.
A ripe plum about to fall.

Nature does not do reverse,
there is only onwards.

Tears that spill.
Earth that claims.
A life now lived.

Absence

You
are missed,
yet no-one speaks of it.

How can we sweep you
under the carpet of our
reluctance to say
your name?

I open the window
and freezing air barrels in.
Everybody comments.

Just testing, I say.

If you crave to talk about the person you lost, and nobody is joining you, you could journal about that person, write a letter to them, record yourself talking about them or to them on your mobile phone or find your own way of honouring them and recognising their existence in your heart, and in the afterlife, if that is real for you (as it is for me).

So many people are inclined to avoid the subject of your loss. Do not let this stop you from continuing your relationship with your loved one! Your heart will not simply stop loving like a tap that can be turned off. Denying the need to love will simply force your emotions underground where they will fester and cause you more problems. In time you will adapt to this new type of relationship... I call it 'loving them from a distance'. Trust your intuition to alert you if you become stuck and need some assistance with this.

Before

I remember when caution
was dust that blew away in
the slightest breeze.

I remember when colours
filled my dreams, hope cleared
my path of all obstructions.

I remember through the haze of
distance. I catch a wisp, hear
the melodies of shadows.

Nostalgia's kisses brush
my cheek.

The past greets me like
a friendly ghost.

Often the well-meaning will say to the grieving, 'you must not dwell on the past'. This is nonsense. Your past may contain beautiful memories. Memories are the treasured possessions of our hearts and minds. They are the most underused things we possess. Visit them to reconnect with the people, the things you have lost. The loss is crushingly real, but not total you see?

Daffodils

Your last request
was for petals.

The luminous
brightness of spring.

How brave
to look the rising
of life in the face,
as yours was fading.

You made forever heroic
for me, those glorious,
golden yellow heralds.

Dinner Party

I take my smile and dust it off,
I polish with a lint free cloth
my witty repartee.

I press my dress, put on my heels
I wonder how the hostess feels
to be inviting me.

I drink some wine, I say I'm fine
I muddle through until it's time
to most politely flee.

We are lonely at home. We are lonely at the party. Grief sometimes feels like a lose-lose situation. Loneliness is asking us to communicate authentically, but we may not be ready to. We may have lost the person that we used to share our most intimate feelings with. Adjusting can take a very long time – finding a compassionate friend or trusted person to talk to is vital as this will provide some intermittent relief.

Cold Spell

Winter suits me.

I scuttle under the
dark feathers of
Mother Nature.

I wear the blackness
of the season, and
grieve more easily.

I drive in the dark
and cry if I want to.

Life goes on,
just imperceptibly so.

As we adjust to a new reality after loss, we naturally have less energy to use in our physical life for a while. The healing of emotional wounds uses up our resources. It is so important not to judge yourself harshly for being able to do less during this time. If you can appear 'normal' on the outside, it is easy to miss what is happening within. While a broken bone mends, we protect it in hard plaster and use it less. Consider how we fail to do this for our hearts and minds when we are deeply grieving.

Lido

I lie face down,
sun hot on my back.

There will be tan lines.

I put off the turning over.
Prostrate like this, plugged into
headphones, I could
be anywhere.

I am burning.
I sit up gingerly.
Don my wrap.

Saunter with exaggerated
nonchalance, through the
sea of happy families.

Run the gauntlet that
life has thrown down for me.

I reach the bar.

Perch with cocktail on a high stool.

Make a note to self, regarding next July.

It can be unbearably difficult to see other people enjoying what you have lost or have never had in the first place. Honour the fundamental sadness about these things; allowing it is a sign of self-respect. A heart that grieves should never be told to shut up. Would you close the door in the face of a weeping friend?

Half-Baked

They say there are five
stages of grief.

A neat recipe, after
which, might I rise like
a triumphant soufflé?

My grief is a wild thing
that will not be captured,
sliced and made sweeter.

It laughs at five, splits
itself into millions.

I will need a
bigger bowl.

Origami

I am turned in on myself.
The deft hands of loss have
flipped and folded, flipped and folded,
flipped and folded me into a strange shape.

I cannot see what
I am meant to be now.

Can you?

It's Time

I'm bagging you up.
Putting your possessions into piles.
Sorting and sifting things you loved,
for strangers to buy.

'They are only things'
someone says, trying to help.
I would throw your favourite novel
at them, if I had the balls.

'You can't keep it like a shrine'
comes another quip. I hide your
dressing gown under the bed, and
your trainers in the airing cupboard.

Best intentions it seems, are
the very flimsiest of things.

We can force ourselves through our grief, as the hardy sort would jump into a freezing cold swimming pool, but we are not just going for a swim! We are adjusting to enormous change on every level. While at times we may benefit from a gentle nudge to move us forward, being rail-roaded into something we are not ready for is not helpful and can set us back.

Possessions can be a great comfort. While they are such, they are useful to your heart. 'Not yet!' can be a useful phrase to fend off the well-meaning brigade. Seek help and advice if you do start to become concerned about your ability to let go of things. Trust your intuition.

Embodied

My heart is crumpled.
I feel it beating, lopsided.
At times, it jumps, startled afresh.

My brain struggles.
Meaning twists like a wet fish
in cold hands. I catch nothing
that makes sense.

I drag around leaden limbs.
Marvel at life's dogged determination.
Weep at life's fleeting passage.

The physical impact of grief is real and profound. Stress hormone levels are very high. Taking care of yourself physically is vital. Sleep, nutritious food, very gentle exercise, plenty of baths or showers, clean clothes – look after your body with love and care while it is being flooded with nature's coping cocktail of cortisol and adrenaline.

Further

I wake before dawn
most nights.

The clock bangs its' drum
close to my ear, but I do not look.

Time marches on, wants to take
me with it; drag me kicking and
screaming in the wrong direction.

I stare into the unknown, delaying
tomorrow for a little longer.

The soft blackness is a comfort.

Within it lies the whole
Universe of you.

Sadness

Many of the so-called 'negative' emotions that we experience, are in fact *defences* against the remarkable emotion that is sadness. Anger and despair, fear and other exhausting feelings of resistance to our difficult realities, are a smokescreen concealing what lies beneath. Our sadness is a deep pool, one in which we do not wish to drown.

And yet, sadness is a remarkable thing - a healing state that is little appreciated. So often it does not get the chance to work its' intended magic.

When we allow ourselves to truly feel sadness, our bodies relax. Muscles loosen, tears flow, and our hearts are allowed their freedom to mourn. Sadness creates a sense of inner space and reconnects us both to the world and to ourselves. We soften into a valuable authenticity, one that enables us to access other helpful feelings, such as hope, patience, compassion and humour. It is no coincidence that we can smile more readily after a good weep.

We are though, vulnerable in our sadness. We feel floppy and defenceless for this time. We feel lonelier as we acknowledge the depth of the loss. Sadness asks us to have the courage to trust – to push away the temptation to maintain our prickly barriers and keep ourselves angry and despairing. Our rigidity is an unconscious protective mechanism, but it is only an illusion of strength. It can keep us on the treadmill of grief for a lifetime.

We will not drown in our sadness, but we may have to swim for a long, long way through it. The waves of it will wash over our heads, but they pass, and each time, the shoreline becomes a little closer.

The beauty of sadness becomes beautifully apparent when our feet eventually touch dry land. We look back at how far we have come and realise that without our sadness, we would still be at the very beginning.

~

~ Journal Page ~

Which losses in my life have I been reluctant to face?

What would I say about those losses if I was completely free to express myself?

How have those losses changed me, and how do I feel about the changes?

If I could forgive myself for anything, what would that thing(s) be?

~ Journal Page ~

~ Journal Page ~

Chapter 5

Natural Solace

*Those who contemplate the beauty of the earth,
find reserves of strength that will endure as long as life lasts.
There is something infinitely healing in the repeated refrains
of nature... the assurance that dawn comes after night,
and spring after winter.*

Rachel Carson, Silent Spring

During my travels through loss and grief, I have become increasingly aware of, and comforted by nature.

The world outside reflects the basic and eternal themes of physical life in its' blooming and dying, but also speaks to us in more subtle ways; the weather of our emotions, the unpredictability of what is coming next, the changes to patterns and phenomenon that we thought we knew how to predict; the way that watching birds and animals can bring us so beautifully back into a present moment awareness.

The atmosphere and energies of the natural world can be a profound source of comfort as they reflect back to us our own experiences, helping us to feel more connected and less alone.

The poems in this section are not arranged in order of the seasons. Grief is as unpredictable as the English weather!

~

Storm Song

There is a great wind
through the forest.

Branches crack and fall.
I know that feeling.

To be bent and buffeted by some invisible force.
To be caressed, then torn apart by fate's breath.

Yet, I see freedom.
The sway of limbs dancing, leaves swirling.
Grace in the rise and fall of
surrendering to the flow.

There is wind in the trees,
and I am shown
a great truth.

The Path

I sweep leaves.
Simple movements,
crisp sounds focus
my attention.

I gather the fallen,
make tidy the bronze
November drifts, but beneath
my suburban duty lies a wild
desire to scatter.

I throw them all into
the air, re-creating
natural chaos.

Now the outside
matches my in.

December

Everything is changed
in my winter garden.

Ice makes brittle
all the bravest leaves;
crisp and fragile wafers
cling to branches,
dark as jet.

Some days the gloom
does not lift.

Only the flash of berry
and crimson feathers
remind me life is not
dying, just sleeping.

I brave the cold,
wrapped in wool and
down, for the sting of
flakes upon my cheeks.

Such stillness and silence
in this frozen haven.
My sadness settles with
the snow, lies like a
white peace.

Wings

Little bird.

You have no idea
what you do for me,
with your quicksilver
dips and bows.

Your tiny silhouette
stark against the
morning sky.

Your flash of flight
to another perch,
and then another.

My heart lifts,
is carried off with you.

Bless you,
little bird.

Driftwood

Upon a tide of
wild white horses, under
turning, vast forbidding sky,
ocean currents brought it
here.

Lost treasure.

I claim it, brush it clean,
will keep it well.

My heart swells
to understand this soft grey,
sun-bleached beauty.

Loss can teach us to value things more fully and find beauty in the very smallest things. My house is full of driftwood and pebbles!

Summer Storm

It is hot
and the swallows
are tossed on the great and
wild waves of thunder clouds
and must swoop as best they
can, riding the boiling
rising air.

Rain

A thousand, thousand
drops keep coming.
An endless patter of
tiny heartbeats.

Nature's pulse
is racing.

My face meets the sky;
wet skin, the window
pane of myself.

Empty

I find it in the swag of ivy
that has grown, blowsy and
exuberant along the wall.

A small nest, hollow
and outgrown.

Each tiny twig
and dried stalk of grass,
each woven wisp of moss,
speaks of urgent preparations.

This feather-lined ball
of endeavours, still so fit
for purpose, vacant in
its' success.

I pray for another brood.
For the divine flash of gaping beaks
and warm huddle of naked wings.

Frost

This white, still world
is brittle to the touch.

My breath, my heat,
a cloud.

I watch the life in me,
dancing before my
eyes.

Shepherd

They are waiting,
fleeces dripping from
a long day in the rain.

One lifts his woollen
heaviness on sturdy legs,
to peer over moss
and stone.

Soft eyes seek along
the lane; black ears prick
and turn towards the low
rumble of approach.

He heaves the sack,
shoulders bent against
years of wilderness, pours
their meal with no ceremony,
but counts heads so carefully,

throws dry sacks beneath
the trailer; assures his flock
it will be fine tomorrow.

The Robin

He sees me first.

The notes of his song, and
bright flash of crimson
rescue my attention.

A drowning thing, I burst
to the surface of myself.

His melodies are
air in my lungs.

He sits in the ivy,
and saves me.

Treasure

Small
brown cone
of woodland pine,
some hundred unborn
trees are nestled safe
between your scales;
I wish that I could
plant each one
for you.

Waking

Crescent moon,
arc of silver light in
pastel blue.

Dove-grey mohair
clouds teased across
a still sleeping sky.

White bonnets on
each leaf, lace of
night frost.

Morning
opens softly,
like rose petals.

Dawn

I open the shutters on my heart
and stand quietly in the
early morning sun.

Pansies flutter as the
breeze grows.

A sparrow wriggles
in its' dust bath.

Life, in glorious detail,
coaxes me out
into the day.

March

The sap is rising,
filling twigs. A rush of life
through sleeping limbs.

All is rebirth, renewal.
I want to join in!

This must be the call of the wild.
A time to return. A bursting out of
the cold, dark depths of loss.

The becoming of
my new, next self.

Secrets

They say trees sleep at night
and droop their branches
in the dark, when
nobody sees.

It does not surprise me
in the least; once I hugged
a tree, and it hugged
me right back.

Icicles

Winter has come
in so many ways.

Long nights and
such icy stillness.

Everything I love is sleeping.
Were there ever really roses here?

The sky is full of snow.
My head, a swirl of
memories.

All The White Flowers

Sometimes, the colour is too much
and all the red for love and yellow
for remembrance, all the purples
and the blues are beautiful but
busy rainbow fragments, and
what is needed is the peace
and profound simplicity of
all the white flowers.

~

Sometimes
what is needed,

is the peace and
profound simplicity

of all the
white flowers.

January

There are snowdrops already,
so green-white delicate.

Pioneers of spring, they
nod serenely in the face
of bitter winds.

I need to know
how to thrive thus, in a world
so wintered, my heart must beat
beneath great drifts of snow.

Hafod

Strange green tentacles have
pushed through beds of
brown needles.

Fern fronds uncurl in
new-born reaching for
gentle sunlight.

The air, cool and bracing in
the shade of dark pines,
is winter still.

It waits for dusk, and a
chance to settle in one
poignant last frost.

The moon is a ghost of herself.
She lingers also, as if to witness
these spring splendours.

White wild garlic blooms,
and drifts of nodding bells
echo a blue sky.

I relish a clear view through
birch and oak; this special vista
summer will obscure.

The forest fills and grows
by the hour; this springtime
is but a fleeting miracle.

~ Journal Page ~

What difference does nature make for me?

Do I notice it as much as I could? Could I include it more in my life?

What natural things do I most love?

Was I more connected to nature as a child, and if so do I miss that?

~ Journal Page ~

~ Journal Page ~

Chapter 6

Unheard Voices

Tell me about despair, yours, and I will tell you mine.

Mary Oliver

When we are suffering, we experience internal pressure. Emotional energy accumulates, and we strive to keep it under control. We do our very best not to express it, because we were taught that to 'complain' must somehow mean we are weak, needy or selfish.

The word 'complain' did not originally have such negative connotations. It has its origins in a far more visceral expression of suffering, evolving from words relating to a 'beating of the breast' and 'emitting a mournful sound'. To complain in its' literal sense is simply *to express outwardly, the stress within.*

As babies it was natural to cry out for attention, but as we grew up we were taught to stifle the very mechanism that is meant to bring others to our side. When we are struggling to readjust after loss and trauma, it is often because we have kept quiet many times, believing this is our best and only option.

Sometimes we do not live in a situation that provides us with the right opportunity to express ourselves openly. There may be nobody in our life who is able to hear us with objectivity and compassion. If this is the case, a well-chosen therapeutic setting may help.

We can also learn how to 'complain' to ourselves! Journalling is one remarkably effective way of providing ourselves with an outlet for all the emotional energy that has been bottled up and not yet processed.

The need to rail against life for a while when it has dealt us a horrible hand, is an inherent part of the authentic grieving process, but we can always find someone who has suffered a greater loss than ourselves. In this way, we tend to belittle our own grief. Comparing our situation to others may bring some helpful perspective, but it is likely to be a very brief interlude. Our own emotions bubble back up again.

Identifying and allowing our feelings properly, does not strengthen them – quite the opposite. They originate in our body, moving up and out when we describe them and acknowledge they are there. As we speak or write of them, the energy of an emotion is transformed. We feel unburdened...clearer, lighter, stronger, more resilient, more optimistic and more objective. An honest chat with a close friend, a proper cry in the privacy of our own space, or half an hour writing down everything we are currently experiencing – all these forms of self-expression can have the same mood-enhancing and healing effect.

The fact that *emotional expression is our built-in relief mechanism* gives us a sensible and very practical reason to allow whatever we are bottling up, out!

Above all, don't lie to yourself. The man who lies to himself and listens to his own lie comes to a point that he cannot distinguish the truth within him, or around him, and so loses all respect for himself and others. And having no respect he ceases to love.

Fyodor Dostoyevsky

Some of the poems in this chapter do not pull any punches, as they were written in times of intense suffering. As I read them back now, it is tempting to label some of them 'too negative', but of course, this is my own 'happiness bias in action'. I include them to demonstrate how much freedom we can give ourselves in the form of personal expression, and how transient these feelings are. When given permission to pass through us, they are no more permanent than a summer storm, and they clear any 'emotional humidity' in just the same way.

*I am not afraid of storms,
for I am learning how to sail my ship.*

Louisa May Alcott

In My Face

Please
don't come at me
with the mop and bucket
of your kindness,

to clean away my pain
as if I am a dirty
window.

You offer me
shiny platitudes
that are foil-wrapped.
I can taste your
discomfort.

I do not want
to have to feel better
for you; I am broken
yet you smile as if
I've lost a button.

Please
don't come at me
with the mop and bucket
of your kindness.

Please don't.

Aftermath

When we look at you, and our eyes are
dark with sorrows, and our hands tremble
as we weep, please do not tell us it
will all be okay.

We are grateful for your kindness,
but those words land like tiny
bombs and make us flinch.

It will not be okay you see, not now the
great gods of loss have sent a mighty
storm, and things we loved are sunk
beneath the waves. It is done.
Life will never be the same.

Join us? In one sentence of agreement.
One phrase of compassionate outrage.
One plaintive 'it's horrendous!'.
Such honest comfort that would be.

Can you allow us to lead with our grief,
to set the mood, and break the rules, for a while?

It will not last. The dust will settle.
No doubt we will apologise
profusely for all the fuss.

But we will remember those hours,
those days when you were our champions.
How you flew the skull and crossbones
in our honour, because for a while,
death was all we could see.

Years Later

As a grieving person, may I be so bold
as to take the timetable of grief, and shove
it somewhere the sun doesn't shine?

May I take liberties, mess with the
schedule, and learn to live with this
at my own snail's pace?

Might I be allowed to let my face
match my internal affairs, as it did
in those first few weeks?

Could I dare to request
an extension?

I have not quite
managed to meet
those recovery deadlines.

No pun intended.

Modern life has elbowed out 'grieving space' because it can be a slow process, with its' own timetable, unique to each person. If you are grieving, erase these two words from your mind... 'By now'. Your progress is not an essay that you must hand in by the end of the month. You are adjusting to a cataclysmic shift in your world, for which there are different parameters. You are entitled to take as long as you wish, to adjust in your own way, to this now very different life.

How Am I?

Ripped, the jagged edge of
something torn.

Imprisoned, within this
high-walled stone fortress.

A banshee, wailing in private,
astounded by my own sounds.

Smiling through an
Oscar winning performance.
The show must go on.

Stunned, a tiny bird, slammed into
grief's glass window.

I'm fine, thank you.

Plea

You do not have
to try and fix this,
nor find magical
words for me.

The world is a
lonely place, when
you become a problem.

When we grieve, we are all too aware that there is nothing anyone can really do to make a big difference. Everybody feels saddened and frustrated by the situation. A big problem though, does not necessarily demand a big solution! This is the error of assumption that can cause so much distress to a grieving person, as people back off and keep away, believing they have nothing to offer. A big problem often requires a solution that is the sum of many small things. Tiny gestures over a sustained period of time, add up to create a beautiful patchwork quilt of loving concern.

Forfeit

I think they think
I am fine as I walk away,
but I am not.

As I tear down the walls
I helped to build, I am
crushed too.

I mourn for the lost girl
in her long white dress
and her beautiful
dreaming.

We can grieve intensely when we make life's hardest choices... the ones that force us to change not only our own lives, but the lives of others too. This grief can go unrecognised. We may appear to be in control, when in fact we are choosing either the rock or the hard place, and both situations are agonising in so many ways.

Sleeping Child

While you sleep, with your
peace and innocence all about you,
I am the parent
I long to be.

Provisions

At the supermarket;
vast emporium of earthly treasures.
I gaze blankly at the grand façade,
swallowing up shoppers.

I feed a hungry trolley with my
pound, grateful for the hire of
my retail zimmer frame.

These days a hopeless customer,
I loiter by the carrots as if I've
never seen one before.

I drop yoghurts, and the bottle
of wine meant to calm my nerves,
fingers frozen not by prawns,
but with grief.

So much dexterity called for.
I no longer arrange my goods,
I lob them into a messy heap
of meals for one.

The till...my jumbled items inch along.
The blessed relief of moody checkout girl,
who glowers at me. I glower back
and send her silent gratitude.

Car-park base camp. The boot is only
half-full. Of course it is, but still, such
a great weirdness. I turn up the radio
and escape to Copacabana.

To Be Or Not To Be

There is a silent vigil,
we who grieve must keep,
lest we blunder into normality,
gate-crash happy places with
our hobnail boots.

There is no tidy way
to bare our souls.

Our choice then,
rock or hard place.

Stoic or
suffragette.

Bare-faced lies
or truthful tales
of woe.

The effort to maintain an acceptable outer façade takes its toll. Whilst putting on some degree of an 'act' is a normal phenomenon of everyday social life, when loss strikes, the gap between inner truth and outer appearance widens dramatically. We expect ourselves to be perfectly convincing, worry that we are not, and feel embarrassed should our grief show through.

The human body functions best when we are in a state of 'congruence' – when our outside and inside is the same, when we are just 'being ourselves'. It is so important to have some regular time in which you can stop pretending. Making this a priority will help enormously.

Time Out

We are meant
to soldier on aren't we,
with our best foot forward and all that,
but this is not a war, and anyway,
I am on my knees.

High Street

It's almost comical.
If I was not still trying
not to drown in the deep
end of sadness, I would laugh.
They see me coming and dive into
doorways, into shops they would
never visit, and try to look as if
they need hardware.

They double-back, they look away.
They become engrossed in catch-up
gossip and wide-eyed contact.
Their ooh's and aah's exclude me;
a language I no longer speak,
or comprehend.

I talk to myself instead.
Keep your head up, I say.
Keep swimming.
Keep breathing.

Disappointment in friendships is a recurring theme I hear again and again when working with clients who are grieving. They are bewildered that the people they believed knew them so well, should become so absent and so different. There is shock at the extra loss this inflicts at such a horrendous time. I have heard the most dreadful accounts of insensitivity over the years! If grief was less of a mystery, supporting each other with simple loving kindness could become a more integral and fulfilling part of our relationships.

The Quietness

It is deafening,
the silence of my hurt.
Call me if you need to, they say.
I do not need to call you,
I need to find you at my door.
The impudence of this grief!

How can I cry out, reach out,
step out into this world?

I am reborn into loss.
Have not yet taken my first breath,
filled my lungs with sharp air.
I can only wait, helpless, hoping.

Call me! they say, and the vice
of pride clamps my lips firmly shut.
My grown adult insists I must
not make a fuss. I can cope.
I can manage. I am strong.

All lies.

Call me if you need me, they say.
I need you, oh I need you!
If only hearts had ears.

Misplaced

It is so convincing,
this illusion of alone.

This sense of being
separate, invisible.

Am I stranded on a
high peak, with wet fog
rolling at my feet and the
wind pulling me to pieces
with icy fingers,

or in the slick, lost depths
of a black cave, that swallows
my cries and holds the echoes
to ransom, so even they can
not come for company.

Or am I the last red berry,
clinging stubborn to a twig
atop a branch they could not
reach, so left instead for
hungry birds.

I wander the aisles
surrounded by trolleys.
Or at least, I think I do.

Elephant In the Room

I park you in the corner.
It's handy you're invisible,
any old corner will do.

Just not over here.
There's no room at this
table for dead people.

I sit here, with my sweep
of pink lippy, and my hair all
blow-dried, listening like a pro.

Julia's grandkids are thriving!
Paula's daughter has just graduated!
Lisa's son is getting married!

I fiddle with my napkin
and very, very quietly
sip my tea.

Not Today

Despair woke me this morning.
Shook my shoulder yet again.

It whispered in my ear,
'Don't get up!
Cancel your plans!...
It will be so much easier.'

I am sick of this voice.
It sounds so like my own
that for an age, I listened
and obeyed.

My anger is useful now.
Propels me, in my fluffy
boots and dressing gown.
I march downstairs like
Boadicea in cream fleece.

I make blueberry pancakes
for breakfast and eat
them outside, in early
morning sunshine.

They taste absolutely
bloody delicious.

Appointment

It is not okay to sit
and scream at
your G.P.

So, I cannot truly
tell him how I'm
feeling.

I can only nod, mute
and compliant as he
whizzes along.

He waves a prescription
at me, as if I have won
the lottery.

I collect my pills.
They are dark blue.
How appropriate, I think
as I sign on the dotted line.

Writing a letter to take with you, explaining your feelings to your G.P. can solve this conundrum very well. No need to scream, nor find the words, nor sit in silent defeat...

Soapbox

I wish to speak the unspeakable.
To broach the forbidden subject.
To wade in and upset the apple cart
if that's ok with you.

I do not love life.

I do not even like it much just now.

Wonderful things happen.
Beautiful things are everywhere!
Then the shit goes and hits the fan.

I understand that it is unavoidable.
I comprehend the cycle of life.
I can self-medicate with objectivity.

But I do not love life.

I tolerate it, as best I can,
wearing this strait-jacket of taboo.

When loss slams into our life, off fly our rose-tinted spectacles. Though we miss them, and wonder who on earth we have become, we can find our way back to peace and appreciation by allowing ourselves passage through a 'natural retaliatory rage' at life, understanding that our self-defence mechanism needs to rise and roar. Connecting with our innate 'fight' helps us to heal, by proving to our unconscious mind that we are not helpless, despite what has happened...

Unwrapped

Life is a gift.
Yes, yes I know.
But it is also the hideous jumper
that you will never wear, the chocolates
when you are on a diet, the bungee jump
gift voucher when you are terrified of heights.

Life is a gift.
Might I have the receipt please?

Fair Weather Friends

It's too dark for them now.
I am too waterlogged for them
to plough a furrow through my pain.

It's too quiet for them here.
Too strange for them to sit in the
weird silence, passing tissues.

They have vanished.
No doubt they do not realise
how they magnify the void.

I am thrown to the lions.
I grab a chair, try to dodge claws,
but this is not a job for one.

Anomaly

I stare into the friendship void;
the strange black hole that
swallows people.

Were they sucked in
kicking and screaming,
or did they jump?

As we feel bitterly disappointed and bewildered when people stay away, it can help to remember they may well be sitting at home feeling the very same way about us, for reasons of their own. Such is the poignancy of disconnected human life in this 'civilised' world! We know so little of each other's inner worlds.

We can be so very thankful for the people who do reach out and offer support. They are a lifeline...angels in disguise- rarer beings who defy modern convention and possess the ability to look the darker realities of existence squarely in the eye. They are usually self-effacing and unaware of their sublime skills!

Winter Solstice

Loneliness prods me with
a sharp stick, urging me to
find you, and of course,
I cannot.

I want to tell you something.
Show you this. Ask you that.
And I cannot.

It is true that in grief, one
becomes a hollow shell.
I am a tree with no leaves.
I am a formless drift of
windblown snow.
I am a barrel full
of cliché's.

Loneliness is dark,
like December.
But Spring will come,
you would say to me.
Just be patient.
Spring will come.

Outrage

How dare life
take you away
when you didn't
want to leave.

I hate that there
are no words to
express this -
thing.

Despairing?
Grief stricken?
Shell-shocked?

No.

I cannot capture
screams in syllables.

My heart thrashes
like a beached fish
gasping for breath.

Nobody throws me
back in.

They smile kindly but
don't look behind my eyes.

I have turned away from
the mirror too; from
the damned truth.

The Card Shop

Here are stacked in
jolly rows, all peeking
greetings of goodwill
and bonhomie.

I am assaulted by
pink elephants and
cupcakes; my throat
tightens, tears prickle.

Here is our corner,
hidden at the back.
The muted colours of
loss. No exclamation
marks to be seen.

Where are the giant
cards of condolence?
Who decreed that grief
is soft and pastel coloured?
Will a moonlit lake do the trick?

I find instead, a quizzical
ostrich draped in a
feather boa.

You will understand
when you open it.

This dreadful nonsense
that is our loss.

The world keeps turning, people go about their usual business, and this can be very hard to bear at times. Losing my Dad when he was so young, for instance, means that every Father's Day is extra painful, and of course, it is a lifelong affliction.

Everyone has their own particular 'Ouch' days. Often there is a build-up to the date, during which emotions can be especially turbulent. Identifying those days in advance and acknowledging your need for self-compassion and care at such times can make a real difference, as can talking about it with someone you trust, and marking the day in your own way.

In Control

I wrestle my anger into
submission, chain it to a wall,
but still it screams up
from the cellar.

I plug my ears with cotton wool,
play loud music, get drunk and
booze happy. Pretend it is just the
wind playing under the roof tiles.

Of course, I cannot keep this up
for ever. I flop, and anger rattles
ironmongery with perfect timing.

What do you want? I shout down.
To talk to you! it shouts back.
Which isn't at all what I
expected to hear.

All our emotions have messages for us. If we take the time to sit with them and listen, they can reveal many helpful things. An intense emotion like anger can feel scary – but in essence it is only a very intense desire to change something.

We do not have to outwardly express the energy of our emotions in their raw and unmanageable form. Anger can be allowed to move within us like a great storm, while we sit completely still. It is the 'squishing' of our feelings into the smallest space possible, the demanding that they be gone, that makes them feel so uncomfortable.

Giving your feelings attention, giving them room and giving them the opportunity to 'speak' – these are the three golden rules of emotional processing.

Resolute

No.
I will not be hushed.
This heart has every right to
love you fully; the memories of you,
the wisps of things we did, even if
they fray at the edges,
weathered by time.

My love for you will grow, not die.

I welcome thoughts of you as they
invade my day, enter without knocking.
I will not push you aside, force you into
some small compartment and bring you out
on birthdays. I will not be told not to dwell
on you, as if you are a problem.

I will rebel. I will roar at them silently, and
defend you to the hilt. I will be your champion,
your advocate, the guardian of your silent presence.

The world will not forget you.
I will love you more, not less.

~ Journal Page ~

What complaints have I never voiced?

If I can express myself with no censoring here, what would I want to say?

If some-one could speak up on my behalf, what would I want them to say?

When are my Ouch days? How can I take care of myself when they arrive?

~ Journal Page ~

~ Journal Page ~

Chapter 7

Blessings

As if we didn't have enough to cope with, even the blessings in our lives can be a tricky subject when we are grieving. We are adrift, in a place so far from happiness that we feel disconnected from lovely things that are happening in front of us. A damping down of our normally appreciative nature is to be expected when we are adjusting to loss. It is understandable, but very disconcerting.

I remember looking out at the garden one April. It was a riot of spring colour and life, one of my favourite things to see. It was so beautiful, but I may as well have been looking at a wasteland. There was no surge of happiness, just a flat-line. I was in the middle of a wave of grief.

There was though, a silver lining. When the wave had passed, I was relieved and delighted to find my appreciation of the garden had, if anything, increased. The writer Kahlil Gibran described grief as that which carves a hollow in our hearts. This same hollow becomes the container of our joy.

This explains perhaps, why over the years, as we process losses, our ability to enjoy life *can* truly deepen.

The ongoing relationship with the blessings in our life can be a helpful indicator of our journey through grief. Enjoyment cannot be forced. Patience is key. Treating ourselves with kindness is essential, especially on the days when a thousand blessings would make no difference whatsoever! If we cannot feel the value of things at the moment, we are *not* ungrateful, nor 'wallowing', nor damaged for ever. There is simply a wave of grief that wishes to move through us…and as we let it be expressed, our connection to the world will right itself again.

~

Following a bereavement, it is also extremely common to feel guilty about enjoying life again. We may worry that any happiness we feel is somehow an indication that we no longer care as much about the person we have lost.

It is important to realise that our hearts have vast capabilities. They can love profoundly, miss and grieve equally as profoundly, and feel joy and delight about something in this present moment, holding all those things within. It is the natural function of the heart to express a wide world of feelings.

Expressing one of those responses at a time does not mean that the others have suddenly vanished.

Enjoy the things you can, when you are able to, and know that your heart is safely looking after your grief and your loyalty and commitment to your loved one. We all need respite. Moments of joy break through to help us cope with our difficult times. Our hearts are far wiser than we know.

~

Gratitude

Your reaching out
with words,

with such kindness
in the question,

is a float, thrown
into the water

in which I am
quietly drowning.

Whilst, with some
exerted effort,

I can probably swim
and save myself,

I shall be lighter
for your concern

and I seize it, grateful,
with both hands.

Affetuoso

Who wrote this music, and how
did they know, so intimately,
the hollows of my heart?

How could they capture the song
of my sadness, as if I had sung it
to them ten thousand times?

The surprise is joy, breaking through,
defying the mood. A melody that soars
and keeps its promises.

Treasured memories sparkle like sunshine
on wild waves and dance before my eyes.

I listen, spellbound, to the
symphony of my grief.

Friendship

You
listen
to me

inviting me
to throw

my words
my thoughts
my fears

into your
well.

Your
acceptance
is so profound

we have
to wait

for long
moments

to hear
the splash

as they
reach the
bottom.

Loved

Sometimes I have nothing much
for you, only the gift of my truth.

Often it is small and not at all
beautiful, and yet it is the only
gift I have.

I wrap it in the finest tissue paper,
ribbons of silk and colours of the
rainbow and hope it will suffice.

I flinch as you open it, for what
can you be, other than disappointed.

But you hold my truth up to the light
and proclaim it the most precious thing
you have ever seen.

Details

All the small things fall into my lap.
Jewels of the day, bright fruits
to be harvested.

The bigger picture has turned
to nonsense. Perhaps I have shrunk.
I do not fit the old world as I did.
Small things are my new foundations.

I am reassured by pigeons,
roosting in the pine.

Cheered by sunlight
as it melts the morning frost.

Comforted by
the humblest cup of tea.

All the small things fall into my lap.
I am lost, but I am blessed.

Seafront

If you were here now
we would sit upon
this bench.

A simple thing; in silence maybe,
listening to gulls cry, or rapt in
the long conversations we
would have, and forget
the world existed.

Our heads bent together
to recount tales, and nod
and laugh at the daftness
of our lives.

We'd pat each other now
and then. That slight touch
that says my heart is full with
you beside me and this is
my subtle thank you.

If you were here now
we would be gazing out
to sea, and pulling tight our
coats in this stiffening breeze.
Memories of a lifetime,
warm me through.

You fill the space beside me
beautifully, as if you never
left at all.

Gentle

There is a bend to me.
I am a willow shoot,
soaked in rain,
grazing the earth.

Heavy with drops that
weigh me down like
crystal jewels,
I am bowed.

You could not make
of me a chair, a table,
or other stalwart,
sturdy object,

but you may weave,
twist and shape me
into a basket, and
I will carry all your
precious things.

Treasure Trove

I used to be careless with my memories.
Would stuff them away like socks in a drawer.

If I had truly known their value, I would
own a thousand diaries, a million photographs.
My mind would overflow with
all the lost moments.

Those I kept, I know so well.
Have played them over, over and over.
Now they leave me craving something new -
some fresh old you please.

I worry. That my mind will toss these
too familiar stories into the trash.
Recycle them without my permission.

I count them in like sheep into a pen.
You asleep in the sand dunes.
You finding my car keys again.
You on a forest path.
Your brown-gold eyes.
Our last dance.
Our very first kiss.

Thankful

That you love the truth of me.
The warp and the shadow of me.
The face I keep turned away
from the world.

That you love the soft edges
of me; those that were lost in the
swirling currents of this life and
are eroded and worn away.

That you love the heavy load my
heart must carry, and reach out
willing arms and shoulder it
for miles when I cannot.

That you love the parts of me
I do not love, and so generous,
include them all in every
warm embrace.

Nursery

There are hands to hold;
a thousand bedtime stories
to be told, and tears to stem
and hair to smooth, whilst
blankets trail and must
be all tucked in.

A million questions every day,
but most remain unspoken
and linger on the rosy lips
of wide-eyed babes.

Time is short and never spare
for moments that would matter so,
and shape small hearts, and
this she sees, she knows.

It is enough somehow,
her love, and shares itself
as loaves and fishes once
fed the hungry bellies of
a watching, waiting crowd.

Empathy

You came
and I had no biscuits,
no teabags and no milk,
so I could not even offer
you a cup of tea.

There was nothing to sip at
as we listened to the clock
ticking, because there was
nothing to say.

Your hand was warm.
I remember that so clearly,
and the deep comfort of
your endless patience.

Gem

You shrug when I thank you,
as if it is nothing, but you do
not bring out empathy like your
best china, only on my worst days.

Your door is always open.
Your heart the same.
This is not nothing.

You are a rare
diamond.

Listening

Sometimes
words fall from my mouth
and drop like lemmings from a
cliff, and crash down onto the
rocks of you.

You who did not ask to be
my jagged shore, but came
in all innocence, to enjoy the
ocean and trail your fingers
through golden sand.

Your love makes
boulders of you, granite
upon which my words can
fall and be shattered into
tiny pieces.

I watch from the cliff top
as the gulls wheel and cry
and I am grateful beyond
measure.

Radiant

Light; it shines somehow through
the cracks of you,

as if your soul can barely contain itself,
and longs to burst out and be seen.

I marvel at how hard it must try
to behave itself,

and stay quiet and good,
like a child at a desk in the
classroom of mortality.

Devotion

I forget to drink my tea again.
You do not mind, not even
by the hundredth cup.

I lose interest in a great movie.
You switch it off and hold
my hand instead.

I go to bed at eight, and read
'til one. You understand the
strange logic that applies.

I shape-shift through my moods.
You stand by, when I am
howling at the moon.

I cry like a small child.
You never, ever, ever
tell me not to.

Unceasing

My heart loved you bigger than itself.

It cannot stop now, that would be ridiculous.
I cannot force the universe back into its' box;
cannot fold up the map of our life together
neatly along the creases.

Our love became a fusion of beautiful regard,
a heady blend of all our sweetest qualities.
It blossomed and burst out all over;
scattered on the wind,
like wild confetti.

This cannot stop now, not for a moment.
I must surrender; allow my heart to love you.
Let it shine into the high heavens.

My devotion mingles with the stars, will gild
the edge of planets, travel to the far reaches
of wherever you are now.

My heart loves you bigger than itself.
Love cannot be contained within these small walls.

Harvest

Loss comes.
I wish it had not.

It comes again.
I wish the same.

For years this is
my story.

One day I look back,
to catalogue all that
has vanished.

I see, not a void, but a
heap of learnt things.

Those stumbles in the darkness
were my falling over truths...

Value is always here, if we can see it.

People are incredible. Mysterious, unfathomable and a constant surprise.

The future is not designed to come sooner.
The present is to be savoured, now.

Loss is survivable. Fear is a test.

Kindness is an antidote to grief.
Honesty is an antidote to grief.
Courage is an antidote to grief.
Humour is an antidote to grief.
Patience is an antidote to grief.

A deep well of compassion lies within every heart. Some just have lids on.

Everyone has met with loss.
Every loss is a personal mystery.

The light and the dark are non-identical twins and cannot be parted.

We descend to the darkest depths but can surface again, many times.

We can crumble and be next to useless one day and be utterly resilient the next.

Panic achieves nothing and is exhausting and pointless.
Panic sometimes must come, and spit and spin for a while.

Life is in control. It is wise to go with the flow.

The heart is trustworthy, even when it is hurting.
The head is sometimes right, but often wrong.

Our bodies can clearly us what they need.

Grief knows where it is taking us.
We should hang on for the ride.

Love is just as powerful from a great distance.

It is Love, LOVE!
that makes it all worthwhile.

~ Journal Page ~

What brings me the most joy?

When have I struggled to appreciate things and why?

Who do I want to thank, and what would I say?

~ Journal Page ~

~ Journal Page ~

Chapter 8

Faith and Spirituality

Should you shield the canyons from the wind storms, you would never see the beauty of their carvings.

Elizabeth Kubler-Ross

When loss sweeps through our life, strange things happen to our spiritual beliefs. The roller-coaster of grief will test our faith in God, destroy it, create it, strengthen it or a peculiar mixture of all these things.

It can be bewildering, but it is understandable, considering the enormity of the challenges that great loss brings. Being forced to look loss square in the face will test our current view of life as profoundly as a hurricane tests a building. All may be razed to the ground, or miraculously, the structure may survive, even if it needs major repairs. Often as we journey through grief, we rebuild our beliefs in a different form.

Life is constant change of course, but loss pushes us, often *forces* us to change. It flips us into a deeply unpleasant new reality – one we would most likely never to have chosen. It is natural that we will then ask *why?* It seems nonsensical. Loss presents us with huge questions we simply cannot answer.

Faith and spirituality, with their meaning personal to each individual, can help us to live alongside those questions with a little more trust and acceptance in our hearts.

My own life-long sense of the spiritual aspect to existence has phased in and out over the years. At times it has been a profound help. At other times I have felt spiritually alone, aware only of being a human being, working my way through this physical reality.

I have come to see that the waxing and waning of my spirituality is as natural as the fluctuation of life itself. Loss shows up everywhere. It makes complete sense to me that there must be times then of spiritual disconnection, when I am left to my own devices. At other times I can acutely sense the spiritual and am supported by loving arms I can almost feel. This tends to happen when I remember to *ask* for that help.

Perhaps, rather like a parent must allow a child to fall over as it learns to walk, life/God stands back and allow us to fall too. In our struggles we can grow. Perhaps loss is deeply cruel to be potentially, profoundly transforming. It is somehow a gentler agony, to hope this may be true.

The transformation of a caterpillar into a butterfly is so often used as a metaphor for personal growth. It is doubtful that any caterpillar, happily munching its' way through a tasty cabbage patch, would ever *choose* to become a chrysalis. Within its cocoon, the caterpillar turns to mush. All that the caterpillar was, disappears into just a gloop of butterfly potential. Life rearranges the physical in a radical, quite 'unpleasant' way, to create something new.

As we grieve, perhaps we are wise to allow ourselves to collapse somewhat. To fall apart; to trust that life can and will rearrange things if we trust it to. And rather like the caterpillar, perhaps we will emerge from our own gloop with colours and new abilities that we could never have imagined of ourselves before.

The Longing

There is a dream of freedom,
and sweet notes from the song of it
blow in on the breeze.

There is a piper on a hill,
in that far off place. He plays the
haunting tune we all remember.

We lean towards it with a strange
ache of heart and fathomless depth
of gaze and strange otherworldliness.

We do not dare to mention it, even as
we all stop to listen, as if the dream of
freedom is our own private mystery.

Persuasion

My soul gently
prised open my fingers

and said 'release this'

and I didn't want to,

so my soul showed
me a future,

and in it I was bent
and twisted

as a gnarled old oak.

The End

I do not cry
when they part,
in those old movies
of a grand love,

but I weep
when they are reunited,
and relief bursts the banks
of my cynicism.

Revealed

I listen at last, to myself.
Not to my loud mind, but
to my heart, my soul;
to what whispers
within.

Each truth I meet with the
tender ear of self-acceptance,
breaks open.

There within, another truth
I have not known before.

I see into the golden depths
of life itself, and the eternity of truths
that will open, all for the knowing.

Our truths are not set in stone, but they must remain in their current form when we do not acknowledge their existence. As I wrote this poem the imagery helped me to see clearly, how validating our truths works to evolve our perception of reality. What is true for us today does not have to be true for us tomorrow. In that there is a great freedom!

Vision

You take my hand
and we sit together.
To find you is a dream
within a dream.

How far you have travelled,
to hide within the very
fabric of reality.

Black Trees

All is shed -
the lush, the ripe
the fragrant.

The bare bones are beautiful.
Sheer nakedness and arms,
fingers, pointing into space.
Look they say.
Look!

Moments

Don your soul spectacles
and peer out at the world.

At first glance
all you will notice
are the bells and whistles
and white noise.

Keep looking
and you will see a flash of
something pure; the truth in
a person's eyes or the beautiful
break of their smile.

There it is -
life, cutting through
all the fuss.

A sweet spot, when the
point of it sounds high and
clear as a temple bell.

Weightless

You moved through life
like a stone skimmed
on water.

Like a fish that leaps
and flies above the
tops of waves.

Like a soul who
remembered,
we too have
wings.

Alchemy

He disappeared
before he left.

Somehow the essence of him
curled away like smoke
into the great beyond.

We watched him.
Gradually going
somewhere.

Last Words

Let me step out
of this garment.
I am fond of it,
but the fresh air
will feel so good
against my soul.

Embarking

I dream of an empty boat
alongside another.

Why are there two boats?
I ask the river, the clouds, for
there is no-one here but me.

You must begin alone,
whispers the breeze.

I see that all I
have to do, is row.

Sahara

Every tear
becomes a flower.
Somewhere a desert is a
soft carpet of blooms now, with
velvet petals and bright leaves.

I weep, and sadness brings life,
even as I am falling to my knees.

Every drop of me missing you,
kisses the earth softly, and
beauty grows and grows.

Revelation

I lay, toppled like a tree.
Roots exposed,
speechless.

Listening
properly
at last.

It is true.

There is a still, small voice
that whispers,

all shall be well.

Untamed

It's my soul
I realised

as I stood
in the queue for
stamps, huffing
and fidgeting.

I am not
ill mannered,

just old,
and tired of
pretending

not to be
wild and free.

Irrepressible

We pruned a tree.
Removed the highest branch
that grew, ever more insistently upwards.

For a while, there was a neat spell.

Then came six new branches,
seeking the sky in blatant disregard.

They make me smile, those branches.

I think of you, wreaking such gentle
rebellion in heaven, refusing to be
pruned; bursting and blossoming
out all over.

Earth Song

She is calling me
as she spins; divine gravity
pulls me to her heart, melody of
sand and stone, the lure.

She gave me this gift,
this flesh and bone, to walk upon her.
She smiled with maternal tolerance and
pride for my tottering steps; watched me
learn to stride, to dance.

Waited patiently for me to take flight
and escape, voyaging beyond her,
to inner outer space.

In time, I will return to her gladly,
all I have borrowed, for her weaving
continues; there are new souls
waiting to arrive, bedecked
in all her glory.

Breath of Life

The wind is blowing
and it blows right through me.
I am an empty building, grateful
for the rush of air that sweeps
my corners clean.

The wind is blowing, and it
carries my soul in a lilt of flight.
I am the rise and fall of a cotton-seed
that kisses the ground, then lifts
and drifts away again.

The wind is blowing,
and it tests my true resolve.
I hold on fast, a tiny leaf on life's tree.
I shake and tremble as I thrive, 'till I am
burnished in the glory of the fall.

Shakti

She breathes the wilderness.
She tastes of earth. Her gale-tossed hair
and flowing rags, stream behind her
as she comes.

She howls; wolves listen and reply
but do not trespass, as she scrapes the
soil to hollow me a bed of moss
and covers me with leaves.

She bares her breast. My hunger is for
skin, for comfort, for her wild electricity.
The crackle of her heart pounds the
rhythm of the earth.

I am told such tales. She weaves and whispers
as I nod and drift to sleep, to ride with her
in dreams of midnight moons.

She is divine, an empress, mystic.

I trail in her wake, and learn and learn,
until it is done, and I am free to rise and surge
upon vast waves of light; to circle the earth
in my own wildness.

And still I hear her wisdom,
in profound and precious echoes,
drifting on the wind.

The Sage

"Please, allow your grief.

Would you stop the rain falling? The dark seasons? The stealing in of night?

If you settle into your grief, you will grow.

You will bloom from the dark earth of it and astonish yourself.

Please, trust your grief.

It will sweep you along like a great river.

It comes to carry your heart back home."

Missing Instructions

Welcome to the world.

Before you begin,
please read the following -

Proceed joyfully but with caution.
Loss could arrive at any moment,
in all manner of disguises.

Loss brings with it many challenges -to live
with an open heart, despite its presence;

to value the many blessings of this life,
even though they may be taken away
without your permission;

to know yourself more fully,
each time loss throws down the gauntlet.

Do not hide from loss, nor ignore it.
Be ready for it, but do not live in fear.

In time you will realise that loss can only take from you what you do not own... and what is *truly* yours, loss cannot take, if you do not let it.

Loss strips away from you all that you can afford to lose, even if this seems harsh and cruel.

Loss will walk with you through this life.

Be a gracious companion.
Walk tall on your journey.

Remember, you are truly loved.

~ Journal Page ~

Journalling can be an excellent way of making more space for the spiritual aspect of life. I highly recommend the book 'Writing Down your Soul' by Janet Conner. Spiritual journaling has helped me to make progress through some of the very darkest times of my life so far. Writing with an open mind and a sense of trust in your connection to life/God can be a remarkable experience, and as Janet explains in her book, we do not have to be only positive and loving when we write this way! In our grief we can express ourselves with absolute emotional honesty and yet still find answers and revelations when we might least expect them.

What would I say to God/life right now, if I do not censor myself?

How could God/life support me more, and what would I ask for?

What emotions can I describe, if God/life is a willing and loving witness?

~ Journal Page ~

~ Journal Page ~

Chapter 9

How To Process Emotion

Contrary to popular belief, we suffer not so much from feeling our emotions, but from trying *not* to feel them.

When we experience an intense emotion, we instinctively tighten up around it, as we attempt to minimise our discomfort. It is something we learned to do as very young children. This tightening up means our emotional energy has nowhere to go and is in fact, made more noticeable as we squish it into the smallest space possible inside us. As we do this, our brain registers the discomfort and releases more stress hormones, further adding to the unpleasantness, and creating a 'vicious circle' of emotion.

What can we do instead?

There are many ways to 'allow' emotional energy to move through us more freely, without sacrificing our privacy or our dignity. Various techniques such as E.F.T. (Emotional Freedom Techniques) can be incredibly helpful.

Over the years of developing holistic psychology approaches, I have found that simple focused application of our attention and imagination can transform our internal world in a very short space of time. As we learn to process our feelings as they arise, we no longer have to be so reluctant to face them and suffer the painful consequences of suppressing our natural responses to life.

Below are the instructions for three of these basic processes, created as I worked with clients to find new ways of working through the intense emotions of grief. They have proved to be very helpful for many people. They are simple to use and with a little practice can become incredibly useful in daily life.

*

1. The Football Pitch:

When you notice a strong and unpleasant feeling, stop what you are doing. If you can, sit down for a few moments, and take a few deep breaths.

Allow yourself to feel whatever you are feeling. It is not necessary to name the emotion, unless you find that helpful – simply notice the sensations and experience of the feeling within you.

Now imagine that inside of you is rather like the Tardis, in Dr Who – far bigger on the inside than it looks from the outside. Imagine that inside of you is as big as a football pitch, or some other area that might suit you better, a huge beach or wide-open fields for example.

Now imagine that the feelings you are experiencing have all this room to fill...

Notice how your body relaxes, and the intensity of the emotion reduces. Giving the feelings 'more room' in this way can dilute their intensity very effectively.

This process demonstrates how much more influence we can have over our emotional responses than we may believe to be possible.

2. The Sieve

When you notice a strong and unpleasant feeling, stop what you are doing. If you can, sit down for a few moments, and take a few deep breaths.

Allow yourself to feel whatever you are feeling. It is not necessary to name the emotion, unless you find that helpful – simply notice the sensations and experience of the feelings within you.

Now imagine that your skin is full of thousands of holes. (this is physiologically accurate of course!) and that the emotional energy that is squished inside you can start to diffuse through those holes and out into the space around your body, in the way that mist travels through the air.
Imagine that there is no limit to how far the emotion can move, up and out in all directions, through walls and ceilings, and all solid objects, as far as it wants to go.

As you do this, notice how your body relaxes and how much easier it feels to give the emotional energy 'permission' to extend in this way.

You will find the intensity of the feelings reducing, often very quickly. Continue to visualise or sense the emotion moving out and dissipating as long as you are still feeling the benefit of the process.

3. The Silent Scream

When you notice a strong and unpleasant feeling, stop what you are doing. If you can, sit down for a few moments, and take a few deep breaths.

Allow yourself to feel whatever you are feeling. It is not necessary to name the emotion, unless you find that helpful – simply notice the sensations and experience of the feelings within you.

Focusing on the intense emotions, imagine what *sound* you would make with these feelings, if you were able to do so freely. It is often a scream, a moan, a wail, a roar, or crying/sobbing. Imagine that you can make these sounds as loudly as necessary, to express them properly. This may be far louder than you would be able to create them in real life!

Now imagine that the feelings are making those sounds, and that you are listening to them as they happen.

Hear the sounds in your mind and let this continue for as long as it wants to. After a while the intensity will lessen. Your emotions will reduce in strength too. This process works because in imagining the noise, we are 'using up' the emotional energy, in the same way as a battery can be drained of power.

Repeat the process if the emotion is still strong. Eventually the noise you imagine will seem to change. If you repeat it enough you may get quite a surprise!

~

These three simple examples are just a selection of the many processes that I teach people, enabling them to deal with their feelings pro-actively and efficiently, whilst understanding that our aim should never be to abolish an emotion as a painful nuisance, but to respectfully and compassionately allow it to move freely, in the way it wants to go.

As a wonderful side effect of regularly allowing our emotions their 'freedom', we are rewarded with new insights and 're-frames' about our situation, a lessening of our problematic mental health symptoms, a reduced need to self-medicate with substances, activities and distractions, and an expanded confidence and knowledge of our potential to survive and thrive, even in the face of life's most difficult situations.

If you wish to know more about my work and the benefits of emotional healing, more information can be found on my website - www.cathryndeyn.com

~ Journal page ~

~ Journal page ~

~ Journal page ~

Farewell

...for now, dear reader. Thank you so much for taking the time to read Secret Grief.

I hope you found a special poem. I also hope that you may have been moved to write something of your own and would ask you to consider sharing it with others - I plan to create a page on my website for some more Secret Grief poetry.

We can all be torch-bearers for others during their own dark nights of the soul. We are blessed to know we are not alone in our feelings as we grieve.

For your losses, a salute. It is a salute well earned. While we must make best use of our stoicism and courage during suffering, we can also gently hold a space for our fears and vulnerabilities as they pass through us. Without those softer and gentler qualities, who would we all be?

May the sun shine on your journey through this life, but when it rains, as it will, let there be an umbrella shop just around the corner!

With love, Cathryn

Acknowledgements

Thank You ...

I am so grateful to all those who encouraged me to press on with my poems and gave me such generous feedback. You may not realise how vital this was to drive me forward through my oft occurring times of doubt. Your parts in this venture are far greater than you know!

A special mention to Rachel, Alan, Carol, Helen, Lynn and Susie, Mike, Charlotte, Margaret, Kerin Webb, Valerie Pinheiro, Casey Kochmer, Suzie Gruber, Marianne Broug, and of course, Simon and Shellie Parke.

To my wonderful clients. In the courageous sharing of your most difficult experiences, you have enabled me to understand the grieving process in far more depth than I could ever have done alone and to write from a place of wider perspective.

To those whose books have helped me process so much of my own emotional gloop – Pete Walker, James Hollis, Peter Levine, Robert Scaer and Gary Craig. I wish that I could shake your hands personally and thank you for your guidance and for blazing such a trail for me to follow.

To Mum and Dad, for helping me
to fall in love at such a young age,
with the power and beauty of words.

To Jack and Matthew, for all the lessons
that motherhood brings, your loving hearts
forgiving natures and ability to laugh so readily
at the absurdities of life.

And to Lennie, for your unwavering support and unconditional love. Without you this book could simply never have happened...xxx

*What is life? It is the flash of a firefly in the night.
It is the breath of a buffalo in the winter time.
It is the little shadow which runs across the grass
and loses itself in the sunset.*

*Isapo-Muxika,
Chief of the Canadian Blackfoot tribe.*

#0098 - 180618 - C0 - 210/148/15 - PB - DID2223979